ONE OF
A KIND

THE LIFE OF SYDNEY TAYLOR

ILLUSTRATED BY

RICHARD MICHELSON   SARAH GREEN

CALKINS CREEK

AN IMPRINT OF ASTRA BOOKS FOR YOUNG READERS

New York

Sarah Brenner knows she is One of a Kind.

She has two older sisters, Ella and Henny.

She has two younger sisters, Charlotte and Gertie.

"But I'm the only one right in the middle," she tells herself.

"I'm the only one born on October 30, 1904. I'm the only one turning seven years old today."

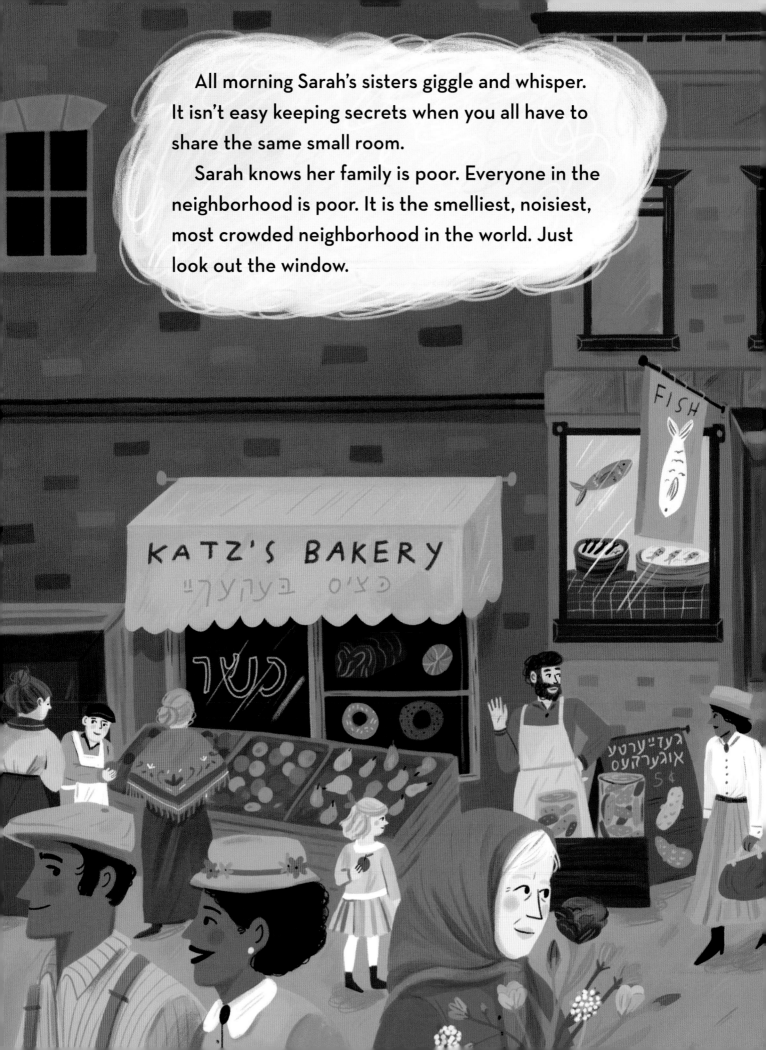

All morning Sarah's sisters giggle and whisper. It isn't easy keeping secrets when you all have to share the same small room.

Sarah knows her family is poor. Everyone in the neighborhood is poor. It is the smelliest, noisiest, most crowded neighborhood in the world. Just look out the window.

It isn't easy making a living. Some poor people collect junk and resell it to even poorer people. That is Papa's job.

"It isn't fair that Papa works from early morning until late at night and we barely have enough to eat," Sarah thinks.
But Mama says today Papa will be home for lunch. With a surprise!

A book! What a luxury. Sarah writes her name—
S. Brenner—on the inside cover. Until now, her
luckiest day was last Friday when she visited the
library. Sarah showed her clean hands, and the
librarian let her bring home *Little Women*, PLUS a
volume of fairy tales. Sometimes Sarah makes up her
own stories and pretends she is a famous author.

"May I borrow a book by Sarah Brenner?" the
other children ask.

Once Upon a Time

Sleeping Beauty

By the time Sarah turns eight, the girls have a baby brother and the small apartment is even more crowded. Mama is always cleaning and cooking or stoking a fire in the coal stove so nobody freezes. Sarah tries her best to be helpful and obedient. She knows life is hard for Mama.

FISH

GROCER

In Europe, Mama had been elegant in her fancy clothes when she attended the theater; Papa had time to carve artistic papercuts. But the German government stole Papa's money and threw him in jail just because he was Jewish.

Sarah's parents wanted a safer place to raise their children and practice their religion. But even in America, good-paying jobs are hard to find. Maybe "happily ever after" endings only happen in books.

Sarah is happiest when the family celebrates the Jewish holidays. Mama and Papa laugh and sing songs. Sarah loves lighting the Sabbath candles every Friday evening. But Mama and Papa encourage the girls to learn American customs, "so you shouldn't feel like foreigners in your own country."

Henry Street Settlement House teaches immigrant families about the Fourth of July and Christmas. There are lessons in how to boil hot dogs and how to use a napkin instead of your sleeve. But what Sarah likes best are the acting and dance lessons.

The theater teacher, Miss Alice, directs political and poetic dramas by modern American writers. The dance classes are run by Alice's sister Irene. Oh, how Sarah loves to twirl to the music! She doesn't have to be a "proper young lady." That's when her body feels completely free.

Happy 4th!

Bread + Butter
NOW PLAYING
by Eugene O'Neill
directed by
ALICE LEWISOHN
Jephthah's Daughter
A biblical dance drama in 3 scenes
by Irene Lewisohn

After class, Sarah walks home. She passes a group of women called suffragists marching for their right to vote.

"Women shouldn't wear pants!" someone yells. "You look like men." "Women aren't smart enough to vote," another heckles. "What's next—a female president?" The crowd begins to laugh.

"Why not?" Sarah thinks. "It isn't fair. I'm as smart as the boys in my class. Shouldn't my opinions matter just as much?"

Sarah decides to start a diary to write down the things she believes in and is too shy to say.

My Thought Book—Sarah R. Brenner—Begun August 1919.

"I have decided to adopt you dear thought book so's I could have someone to tell my thoughts to and these I could never, never as long as I live tell to any living person."

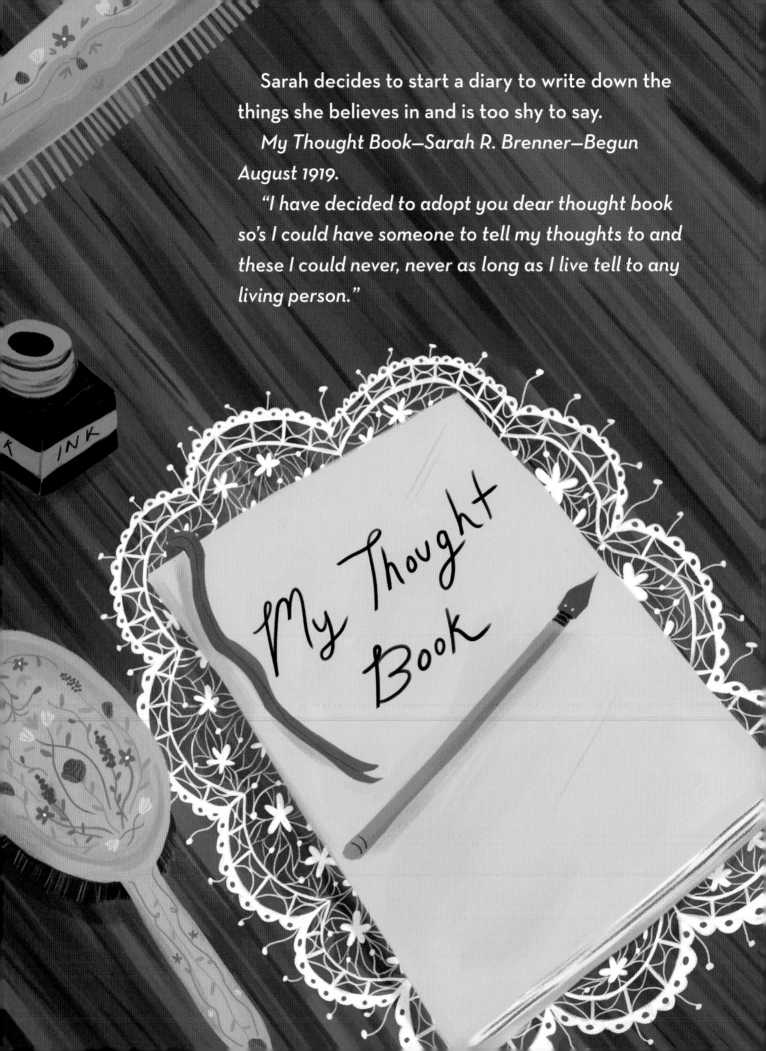

Sarah is fourteen years old. She is tired of being quiet and well-behaved. Boys are encouraged to speak out and be fearless. She decides the name *Sarah* sounds shy and old-fashioned. "I need a modern name, maybe even a boy's name; then people will pay attention to what I write." She signs her next entry, *Sydney*.

Sarah Brenner is now Sydney Brenner.

Morris High is the first public school in New York City to enroll both male and female students, but all twenty-six class representatives are boys. "It isn't fair," Sydney knows. "It's time I spoke out!" She is excited to be elected, and even happier the next year when women win the right to vote in all of America's elections.

Sydney finds a job as a secretary. Because she is blond and speaks English without an accent, the other workers don't guess she is Jewish. One day she hears them complain that all Jews are dirty and lazy and deserve to be poor; the next day the same people grumble that all Jews are rich and trying to take over the world. Sydney is furious.

"It isn't fair to blame Jews, just because we have different traditions," Sydney scolds them. "All people should be respected regardless of their race or religion."

Sydney also knows it isn't fair that bosses are getting rich while most workers aren't paid enough to feed their families. She joins the Young People's Socialist League, a group that fights for higher wages and safer working conditions. At today's meeting Sydney sees a young man named Ralph Taylor. Ralph is just as passionate as she is about equal rights for everyone. And he loves dance and theater. Plus, Sydney notices, he is very handsome.

"We are two of a kind," she tells Ralph. Two years later they get married at city hall.

Sydney Brenner is now Sydney Taylor.

But even though every wife she knows has taken her husband's last name, she writes S. *Brenner* on their apartment door buzzer.

The Lower Manhattan neighborhood where Syd and Ralph live is filled with young people discussing politics and the arts. Syd loves performing off-Broadway with the Lenox Hill Players, and she is even more excited when she gets a chance to dance with the Martha Graham Company. For the next five years Syd expresses her ideas of protest and freedom through the way she moves her body.

But Syd and Ralph have one more dream: to start their own family.

IMMIGRANT, STEERAGE, STRIKE!

THE VEGETABLE
NOW PLAYING!
by F. Scott Fitzgerald

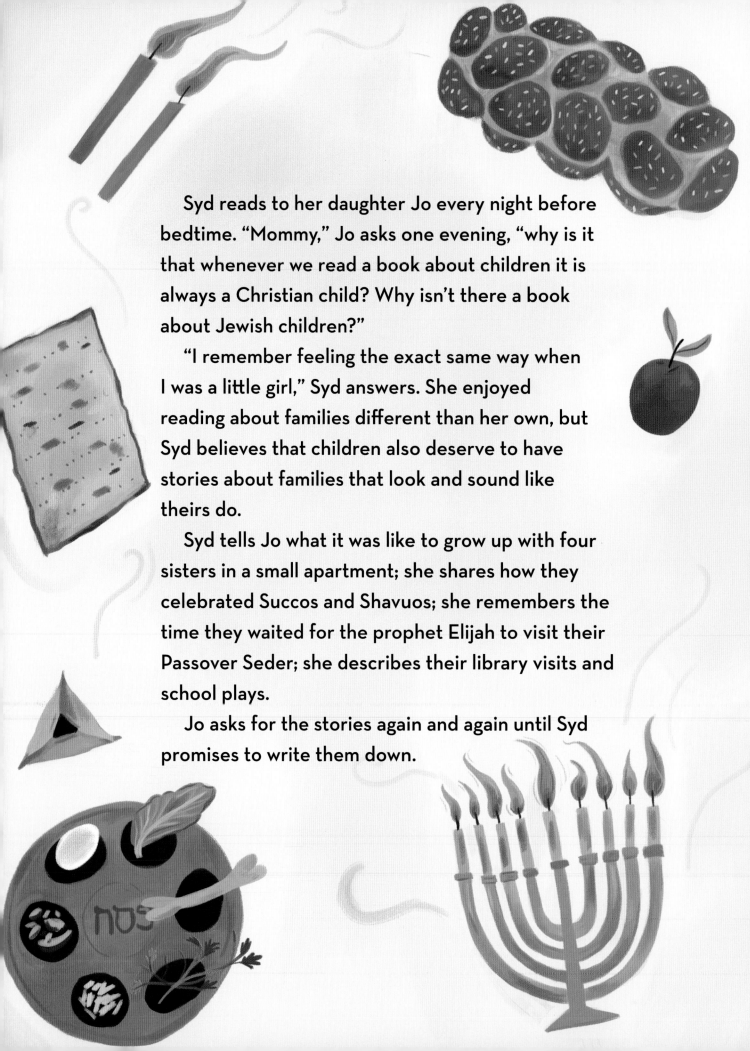

Syd reads to her daughter Jo every night before bedtime. "Mommy," Jo asks one evening, "why is it that whenever we read a book about children it is always a Christian child? Why isn't there a book about Jewish children?"

"I remember feeling the exact same way when I was a little girl," Syd answers. She enjoyed reading about families different than her own, but Syd believes that children also deserve to have stories about families that look and sound like theirs do.

Syd tells Jo what it was like to grow up with four sisters in a small apartment; she shares how they celebrated Succos and Shavuos; she remembers the time they waited for the prophet Elijah to visit their Passover Seder; she describes their library visits and school plays.

Jo asks for the stories again and again until Syd promises to write them down.

Syd is eager to write even more stories and send them to magazines. Maybe her words can help change the world for the better. Maybe she can show other children that all people—whether their family have been in America for generations or are recent arrivals—share the most important things: a love of friends and family and a desire to be treated fairly.

But the publishers don't agree. America is at war overseas, and no one is interested in reading about little girls or refugees or immigrants like Syd's family. Syd stuffs the stories in her dresser drawer and forgets all about them.

But Ralph doesn't forget. Years later, he hears about a contest. A publishing company is offering an award of three thousand dollars for an unpublished book of children's stories. World War II is over, and maybe the world is finally ready to celebrate all customs and cultures. Ralph pulls *All-of-a-Kind Family* out of Syd's drawer and mails it off in a big envelope.

WILCOX + FOLLETT
PUBLISHERS
NOV. 21, 1950
Congratulations!
All-of-a-Kind Family
has won first prize!
Esther K. Meeks,
Editor
COBBLER

What a surprise! A book. It's a happily ever after ending!

AFTERWORD

All-of-a-Kind Family was published in 1951 and was an immediate success. It was the first Jewish children's book to become popular with non-Jewish readers.

Sydney went on to write four more books about her family: *More All-of-a-Kind Family* (1954), *All-of-a-Kind Family Uptown* (1958), *All-of-a-Kind Family Downtown* (1972), and *Ella of All-of-a-Kind Family* (1978). She also wrote and published five other books about Jewish life.

Her books both showed and helped shape American Jewish identity in the twentieth century. While Sydney didn't follow the strict religious practices and rules that her parents did, she infused every story with her values of family love, compassion, and social justice.

Cilly and Morris Brenner with the five sisters Ella, Sarah, Gertie, Charlotte, and Henny, 1909

Sydney served as the dance and drama director of Camp Cejwin, a nonprofit Jewish children's camp, for almost forty years. She wrote many plays and songs for the children, often with the help of her sisters.

Sydney Taylor, 1920s

Sydney helped break down barriers so that all ethnic groups could eventually have a voice in children's literature. Every year since 1968, the Association of Jewish Libraries has presented an annual award to outstanding books for children and teens that authentically portray the Jewish experience.

After her death on February 12, 1978, the award was renamed in Sydney Taylor's honor.

ABOUT RALPH TAYLOR

At age twelve Ralph Taylor got a job as an errand boy at Caswell-Massey, the oldest apothecary business in the country. In 1936, less than two years after Jo was born, Ralph and his brother, Milton, bought the company.

Ralph Taylor, 1920s

He would create perfumes for many celebrities, including actress Greta Garbo. Ralph also co-founded the journal *Dance Observer* with Louis Horst, who was Martha Graham's mentor. Ralph loved baroque music and was a member of the American Recorder Society. He died on June 24, 1993.

ABOUT JO TAYLOR MARSHALL

Syd sent her daughter, Jo Taylor Marshall, to nursery school at the original Bank Street College of Education, known for its progressivism and child-centered philosophy. After Bank Street, Jo attended Greenwich Village's Little Red School House, which promoted progressive politics and an experimental educational philosophy. She graduated from Sarah Lawrence College and Columbia School of Social Work and had a successful career as a social worker, administrator, and Columbia University faculty member. Like her mother, Jo is a devoted fan of theater, film, literature and dance. Jo is now retired and divides her time between Florida and New Jersey.

Sydney Taylor with Jo, 1936

AUTHOR'S NOTE

I grew up in East New York, Brooklyn, in a neighborhood that was rapidly changing from Jewish to African American. My parents were totally secular, and we celebrated no Jewish holidays. Weekends I worked in my father's hardware store. I didn't mind delivering paint, but I hated sweeping—that is until my father dropped some pennies in the dusty corners and under the counters. Very occasionally I would find a nickel or a dime. I could keep what I found, and I became an enthusiastic sweeper.

I did not read Sydney Taylor's books as a child, but that is no surprise as I did not read many books at all until I entered high school. When I won my first Sydney Taylor Gold Medal in 2009, I read the All-of-a-Kind stories for the first time. By chapter two, when Mama hid buttons to entice her girls to do a better job dusting, I was hooked. As a writer myself, I knew Sydney was composing stories, not penning an autobiography, but I loved the rich historical details, and I too wanted to be a part of the Taylor family.

After I was fortunate enough to win a second Sydney Taylor Gold Medal in 2018, I had lunch with Jo Taylor Marshall. She was filled with enthusiasm and shared many of her own stories. I asked about her mom, and Jo's answers brought Sydney to life. I started writing this book the very next day.

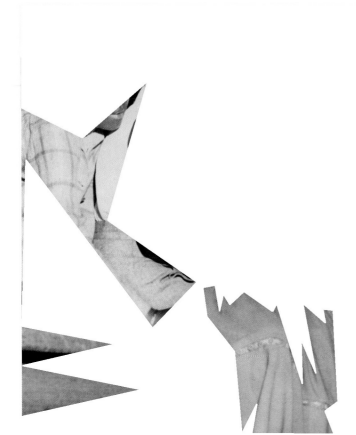

Sydney with schoolgirls at the Hall Branch Library in Chicago, around the mid-1950s

BIBLIOGRAPHY

The words attributed to Sarah's diary in this book are, in fact, taken directly from her diary; and the exchange with Jo about the need for Jewish characters in books is based on a draft of a speech Sydney gave at the New York Public Library in 1961. Most of the other dialogue is invented, but the thoughts, if not the exact words, are all taken from Syd's writings or Jo's recollections.

PERSONAL INTERVIEWS

Dunietz, Alexandra. Email exchanges with the author, February–May 2020.

Marshall, Jo Taylor. Interviews with the author, June 18–20, 2018.

——. Phone interview with the author, July 7, 2018.

PRIMARY SOURCES

Cummins, June. "Becoming an 'All-of-a-Kind' American: Sydney Taylor and Strategies of Assimilation." *The Lion and the Unicorn* 27, no. 3 (September 2003): 324–43.

——. "Leaning Left: Progressive Politics in Sydney Taylor's All-of-a-Kind Family Series." *Children's Literature Association Quarterly* 30, no. 4 (Winter 2005): 386–408.

——. "Sydney Taylor: A Centenary Celebration." *The Horn Book*, March 30, 2005. hbook.com/?detailStory=sydney-tay-lor-centenary-celebration.

Cummins, June, and Alexandra Dunietz. *From Sarah to Sydney: The Woman Behind All-of-a-Kind Family*. New Haven, CT: Yale University Press, 2021.

Taylor, Sydney. Plays, letters, and journals from the collection of Jo Taylor Marshall. Unpublished.

ACKNOWLEDGMENTS

Special thanks to Jo Taylor Marshall and Alexandra Dunietz for supporting this project and answering my many questions. And to Lesléa Newman for years of friendship and for asking, at the 2018 AJL Conference, "I'm on my way to have lunch with Jo and Mase. Want to join us?"

Richard Michelson and Jo Taylor Marshall, 2022

For Jennifer, my One-of-a-Kind lifelong love. And in memory of June Cummins. —*RM*

To the whole of my family, whose story was so much like the one told in this book.
Thank you for the brave choices. —*SG*

Picture Credits

Judy Magid: 36 (left); Jo Taylor Marshall: 36 (right), 37 (both), 38; Richard Michelson, 39.

For information about permission to reproduce selections
from this book, please contact permissions@astrapublishinghouse.com.

Calkins Creek
An imprint of Astra Books for Young Readers,
a division of Astra Publishing House
astrapublishinghouse.com
Printed in China

ISBN: 978-1-63592-531-9 (hc)
ISBN: 978-1-63592-549-4 (eBook)
Library of Congress Control Number: 2023905063

First edition
10 9 8 7 6 5 4 3 2 1

Design by Barbara Grzeslo
The text is set in Neutraface Text Demi and Book.
The illustration medium is digital gouache.